Original title:
Under the Comfort of Snow

Copyright © 2024 Creative Arts Management OÜ
All rights reserved.

Author: Seraphina Caldwell
ISBN HARDBACK: 978-9916-94-402-8
ISBN PAPERBACK: 978-9916-94-403-5

Chill Whisper Beneath the Moonshine

Frosty breath tickles the air,
Squirrels suit up, planning to dare.
Snowflakes giggle, dance in the light,
While rabbits hop, filled with delight.

Tea in cups, steaming like dreams,
Mittens lost to mischievous schemes.
Snowmen sport hats far too big,
Their carrot noses dance a jig.

Chickens wear boots, ready to slide,
While penguins strut, full of pride.
The world wraps in a cozy jest,
As laughter warms every chilly quest.

Moonbeams shimmer, casting a glow,
On snowball fights where kids all throw.
Each chilly skirmish, a giggle release,
In the frosty air, there's pure, silly peace.

Embraced by Crystal Silence

The flakes fall down with such grace,
They blanket all in a white embrace.
Yet here I stand, just one big sneeze,
While snowmen chuckle, bending at the knees.

My scarf is tied in a knot so tight,
That even frost would find no respite.
I strive to frolic, take a grand leap,
But trip over my boots, and into a heap!

Stories Woven in the Flurry

As flakes dance round, they twirl and spin,
I swear they're up to some silly sin.
Whispers tumble from tree to tree,
While squirrels giggle, what could it be?

With cheeks like cherries, I waddle about,
My balance? Gone—my pride's in doubt.
A snowball flies, though I have no aim,
"Is that a snowball fight? Who's to blame?"

Beneath the Quiet Crystal Canopy

The world wrapped tight, a sugary treat,
I hear my boots squelch, a crumby feat.
A giant snowman leers with a grin,
I wonder if he's storing all my sins.

My snow angel looks more like a fish,
A wish, oh please, for a better swish.
I tried to look graceful, but oh dear,
I'm a snowball's target, that much is clear!

Shivers of Glistening Serenity

The air bites quick, it's quite rude,
While frozen fingers stitch my mood.
I laugh and cough, then slip with flair,
Like a comedian on a snowy prayer!

Sledding downhill, oh what a sight,
Left behind is my dignity, light!
Fatigued by laughter or just a bit cold,
These snowy days never grow old.

Secrets Linger where the Ice Glows

Fluffy flakes dance, a whimsical sight,
Snowmen giggle in the soft moonlight.
Their carrot noses, a comical take,
They whisper secrets, oh what a mistake!

Sleds zoom by with squeals of delight,
While hot cocoa spills under a starry night.
Frosty breath puffs like dragon's breath,
Laughter wraps us like an icy wreath.

Journey Through the Winter's Embrace

Bundled up tight like a burrito roll,
Ice skaters spin like they're on a stroll.
Snowball fights make cheeks all aglow,
Who needs a gym? We're pros in the snow!

Hats fly off in the frigid breeze,
Chasing them down like we're trying to tease.
Slip on a patch, land right on your rear,
We laugh so hard, can't help but cheer!

Memories Encased in Frosty Gleaming

Twirling snowflakes weave stories so bright,
In the white blanket, everything feels right.
A snow-dog barks, chasing shadows all day,
While I trip on my laces and fall in the spray!

Kids create angels, pure joy in the air,
Like fluffy marshmallows, they float without care.
One cheeky snowball sneaks right past my face,
"Revenge," I plot, as I quicken my pace.

Frosted Reflections of a Silent Heart

Frozen ponds hide what they can't say,
But snowflakes giggle and dance in their play.
Each chilly breath puffs clouds of delight,
As winter surprises, oh what a sight!

With boots that squeak like a rusty old door,
I waddle and slip, who could ask for more?
Laughter erupts in a flurry of fun,
We embrace winter's charm, oh, how we run!

Frost Kissed Reminiscences of Night

When snowflakes fall and coats are tight,
I slip and slide, what a funny sight!
A snowman grins with a carrot nose,
As laughter echoes through frosty prose.

A snowball fight breaks out in a dash,
With flying fists, oh what a clash!
But then I trip, and there I lay,
A frosty beard in the light of day.

Twilight Dreams Wrapped in White

Twilight drapes the world in lace,
Slipping on ice, oh what a race!
A sled goes flying, a cheer we hear,
As someone ends up wrapped in gear.

With cheeks so pink and noses red,
Making angels in the snow instead.
I think I saw a yeti too,
Turns out it's just my friend with glue!

The Soft Echo of Falling Snow

Whispers of snowflakes dance in the dark,
As squirrels plot their winter park.
A snow-covered branch breaks with a splat,
Down goes a cat, and how about that!

The sidewalk's a canvas, bright and clear,
As I walk, I begin to veer.
My footprints zigzag like a lost kite,
A map of mishaps in winter's bite.

Traces of Light Beneath Winter's Veil

Winter's cloak pulls tight with glee,
I slip on a patch, oh dear me!
A tumble, a roll, then I see stars,
Was that a tumble or a dance of Mars?

Snowball clump and a chilly grin,
I launch it high, let the fun begin!
But watch out, friend, you're now this year's,
The target of laughter and joyful cheers.

The Gentle Enchantment of Snowflakes

Snowflakes giggle as they dance,
Frosty socks are lost by chance.
The chilly breeze gives a tickle,
Watch out, here comes a snowball pickle!

Kids in coats that make them wide,
Slide around with snowy pride.
But dad slips down, what a sight!
He claims he's graceful, but oh, what a plight!

Snowmen talk with carrot noses,
Making friends with frozen poses.
But one has legs that walk away,
Guess he didn't like the snowy play!

The winter sun gives a sly grieve,
While hot cocoa's hard to believe.
Snowball fights and laughter bright,
In this wonderland, we take flight.

Phantom Footsteps in the Winter's Glow

On winter paths, strange sounds abound,
Phantom footsteps? What's that sound?
It's Grandma's cat, she's on the roam,
In mittens lost, she finds her home.

A snowman waves with a crooked grin,
"Wanna race?" he shouts, oh, where to begin?
Sleds tumble down, what a wild thrill,
Who's steering this? Not me, what a chill!

Walkers hop, avoiding the drift,
In snow boots squeak, they slide and lift.
Hot cider spills, there's no time to waste,
Laughter fills the chilly space!

At night the moon shines, oh so bright,
With snowflakes dancing in pure delight.
While we laugh till we drop and neigh,
Winter shenanigans are here to stay!

Dreams Drift on Whispering Winds

Dreams drift soft on chilly air,
Jingle bells ring, a festive flare.
Sleds become rockets, soaring high,
"Oh, dear stars, look, I can fly!"

Snowflakes whisper silly tunes,
While snowmen parade with laughter balloons.
In hoodies bright and scarves that twist,
They mingle and dance, you get the gist!

Grandpa's snoring as snow falls thick,
"A snowball fight?" Oh, that was quick!
He jumps awake, a startled sight,
Bursting into laughter, what pure delight!

As dusk falls down, the world aglow,
With all the joy wrapped in the snow.
We share our dreams, sparkle and cheer,
For winter's magic brings us near.

When the World Becomes a Shimmering Dream

When the ground is dressed in white,
We gather 'round for pure delight.
Giggling friends and frosty cheer,
Comedic slips, no worries here!

Toboggan rides are quite a blast,
With spins and flips that happen fast.
Mom lost her hat, it flies away,
Chasing shadows in disarray!

Snowball battles break out with glee,
"I'll get you first!" then "Oops, was that me?"
Fluffy clouds conspire to tease,
While snowmen crack jokes with frozen ease.

As the evening blankets the light,
We revel in this winter's night.
With laughter echoing through the gleam,
The world is magic, like a dream!

Reveries in the Soft White Glow

Snowflakes dance like little clowns,
Tickling noses and cozy gowns.
Every snowman looks quite absurd,
Waving sticks like a quirky bird.

Children laugh, their cheeks like red,
Launching snowballs, aiming for heads!
Sleds go flying, oh what a sight,
It's a blizzard of giggles tonight.

Serenity Amongst the Winter's Veil

In a dream of white, I stumble and trip,
Caught in a snow drift, my pants start to rip!
Hot cocoa spills, oh what a mess,
Marshmallows float like a fluffy dress.

Penguins strut in the icy glow,
Wobbling with style, putting on a show.
Nature's joke with every flake,
Making snow angels, with each silly shake.

Guardians of the Silent Frost

The squirrels wear jackets; they look so grand,
Chasing each other, doing a stand.
The moon chuckles, casting its light,
While I slip on ice, what a comical flight!

Trees wear hats made of heavy snow,
Whispering secrets that only they know.
Frosty wind sings a frolicking tune,
As I flap my arms, looking like a loon.

A Tapestry of Snowy Silence

Puppies tumble in soft, fluffy stuff,
Paws going everywhere, oh it's so tough!
Building snow forts, like castles of play,
Till a snowball fight sends them on their way!

Gossiping snowflakes gossip with glee,
"Who wore it best?" they giggle with me.
In the winter's embrace, we find our cheer,
Wrapped in laughter, we dance, we veer.

Nature's Softest Lullaby

The flakes fall down like lazy cats,
Dressing roofs in fluffy hats.
Squirrels glide on tiny sleighs,
Wondering how they'll spend their days.

No need to rush, let plans be late,
As snowmen march, they'll celebrate.
With carrot noses, cheeky grins,
They'll plot the best of snowy sins.

In winter's grip, we laugh and play,
Chasing each other in a snowy ballet.
While cocoa waits, all frothy and warm,
We'll dance 'til dawn in our winter charm.

Fragments of Frosty Reverie

A snowball fight erupts in cheer,
Missed in flight, oh dear, oh dear!
A hat flies off, the laughter grows,
As cold noses get warm with blows.

The dog runs wild, a fluffy blur,
Chasing the kids - what a stir!
With every leap and woofing sound,
Joy ricochets all around.

Hot chocolate spills on winter boots,
Sticky marshmallows make sweet hoots.
With each slip and tumble and fall,
We giggle and grin, love conquers all.

A World Paused in Crystal

The world looks like it took a nap,
With blankets white, oh what a trap!
Icicles dangle from each eave,
Smiling at the trouble we weave.

Penguins in scarves make quite a scene,
Shuffling about with some bean machine.
Snowmen plotting with twinkling eyes,
Dream of snowball grenades as the prize.

The car does a slide, not quite the goal,
The driver turns pale, losing control.
But laughter erupts, no road rage here,
With snowflakes falling, let's all cheer!

Shadows Dance on Wintry Days

The shadows stretch as sunlight plays,
While little critters prance and sway.
A rabbit hops, then takes a bow,
Waving to the snowman, oh wow!

A penguin in boots feels quite absurd,
Trying to fit in with a flurry of birds.
He flaps his wings with comedic twist,
Imagine the headlines: 'Penguin Dancer Missed!'

Snowflakes tumble like jokes on cue,
Each one unique, a puffy debut.
As laughter wraps around like a scarf,
Winter's wild wit sparks every laugh.

Frosted Hush of Evening

Flakes dance down, a winter's waltz,
Cats chase shadows, not caring at all.
Noses red, cheeks like cherries bright,
Snowball fights make the evening light.

Mittens lost, a comical sight,
Sleds flip over, what a wild flight!
Laughter echoes through the blanket white,
Hot cocoa spills, oh what a delight!

Frosted eyebrows, friends all aglow,
Tripping on toes, who's winning? Oh no!
Each snowman leans, a crooked grin,
As evening wraps us, let's dive in!

So let the flurries come tumbling down,
In this playful joy, we wear our crown.
Unexpected slips and frosted fun,
We greet the night—let the laughter run!

Secrets of a Snowy Slumber

Pillow fights in the frosty rooms,
Feathers fly like tiny flurries blooms.
Blankets piled, a fort so secure,
Laughter lingers, what's life without cure?

The cat sneezes at the sudden stir,
While dreaming of fish, he gives a purr.
A snowman's nose made of carrot delight,
Eats up my cookie! Oh, what a fright!

Hot soup waits, but we're lost in joy,
Launching marshmallows like a kid's toy.
Found a snowball tucked in my coat,
Oh dear! Was that a flying goat?

As night settles, the world is still,
But in our hearts, the giggles thrill.
Beneath the moon, secrets take flight,
In winter's lull, we find our light.

The Embrace of Wintry Stillness

Whispers of quiet, snowflakes sing,
Characters frozen in winter's bling.
What's that? A snowman with a hat?
He's wearing sunglasses! Imagine that!

Sneaky squirrels bound through the trees,
Sliding down branches, with utmost ease.
Daring the dogs to join in the chase,
They tumble and roll, oh what a race!

Snow forts built like majestic towers,
Too much fun, we forget the hours.
Our cheeks puffed up, can't help but pout,
It's just a snowflake! Oh, watch out!

Stars glow high, winter's fancy dress,
In these still moments, we laugh and bless.
With hearts so warm in the frosty chill,
Let's embrace this warmth, laughter's our thrill!

Feathered Silence on the Ground

Downy feathers float, whisper soft,
Tumbling snowflakes craft a cozy loft.
Baffled by boots that slip and slide,
A snow angel giggles, our joy can't hide!

Gather your pals for a snowball court,
Noses at red, what a snowy sport!
Socks mismatched, who needs a pair?
Winter's folly, with nary a care!

Ice cream trucks in a blizzard parade,
Scream for ice cream, oh what a charade!
With each playful push and snowy shove,
Laughter erupts, our tiresome love.

So come join the fun as the stars twinkle,
Chasing laughter, we dance and tinkle.
With the night whispers, we laugh and shout,
In this snowy dream, we're full of clout!

Mysteries Hidden in the Frosted Light

The snowman argues with a tree,
His nose a carrot, can't you see?
He claims he's warm, but feels the chill,
Best stick around, or he'll get ill.

The rabbit hops with fancy flair,
His ears are tucked, but oh, what hair!
He tells tall tales of winter's tricks,
As fluffy clouds give him a fix.

The icebergs dance with giddy glee,
Sipping tea with a frosty bee.
The sun peeks out to join the fun,
But snowflakes laugh, 'We're not yet done!'

A snowflake giggles as it falls,
Whispers secrets through snowy halls.
Each flake a story, so divine,
In frozen laughter, we all align.

The Peace of a Whispering Winter's Night

The night is calm, or so they say,
But snowballs lurk in clever play.
A squirrel chases, thinks he's sly,
His frosty tail waves goodbye.

The moon shines bright on rooftops white,
While penguins waddle, what a sight!
They slide and slip with giddy yelps,
While snowmen cheer for winter's kelps.

A snowman dreams of beachy scenes,
Donning shades and daring routines.
His snowball pals all roll their eyes,
"Just stick to this, ya frosty guys!"

Snowflakes skate with twinkling grace,
In a chilly waltz, they find their place.
Each flurry seems to join the fun,
Chasing shadows until they're done.

Lifting Veils of Frozen Dreams

The icicles dangle and they sway,
Whispering secrets of winter play.
They tease the wind, "Come join our song,"
As snowflakes giggle, short and long.

A sleepy bear in white coats spun,
Awakens to find that snow is fun.
He tumbles, rolls, then strikes a pose,
Stuck in snow, just like his toes!

The snow creates a magic sphere,
Where penguins slide and shed their fear.
They plot a snowball fight with flair,
Wings flapping, flying through the air.

Beneath the snow, a world concealed,
With frosty fun, the fate revealed.
In frosty laughter, dreams arise,
Each chilly moment, a sweet surprise.

Enchantment in the Snowy Silence

In silence, giggles sprinkle down,
As winter wears its gentle crown.
The rabbits gather to exchange,
Their fluffy tales, a bit deranged.

A gentle breeze begins to tease,
A snowflake lands upon the leaves.
It whispers, "Hey, I'm fancy frost!"
While snowmen claim, "We're truly lost!"

The owls hoot softly from the trees,
Their laughter woven with winter's breeze.
A snowstorm's dream of Noel's dance,
Twinkling starlight, a fleeting chance.

In this frosty, silent spree,
Where every snowball wants a spree,
The winter chuckles in delight,
As we all dance through snowy night.

Echoes of Stillness on a Frozen Morning

Icicles draped like fancy hats,
A snowman dances and spouts chitchats.
Squirrels glide in fluffy suits,
Doing pirouettes in snowshoe boots.

Tea's gone cold, I blame the frost,
My morning toast? Now a snow crust.
Pancakes flutter like fallen leaves,
Breakfast waits, but winter thieves.

Each step I take, a crunching sound,
Soundtrack of clumsiness all around.
I stumble, slip, then start to laugh,
Snow won the duel—what a funny staff!

Voices echo in the frozen air,
Where even snowflakes stop to stare.
Jokes are whispered on the breeze,
Nature's laughter, if you please.

Tales from Beneath the Icy Canopy

Penguins slide with utmost grace,
A snowball fight breaks out in space.
The laughter lifts like clouds aglow,
As powder puffs get tossed just so.

Fluffy white on every porch,
Hiding puppies, oh what a search!
The cat just pouts, royal and proud,
While snowflakes dance, mischievous crowd.

Behind the trees, a stealthy sneak,
A snowman giggles, making a peek.
With buttons made of cola caps,
The fun begins, no time for naps!

A hot cocoa spill, oops, what a sight,
Swirls of marshmallows in the moonlight.
We'll tell our tales to nature's cheer,
Of frosty mornings bright and clear.

The Beauty of a Secret Snowfall

A quilt of white, the world's asleep,
Laughter muffled, secrets keep.
Snowflakes tumble with joyful flair,
Spring's not here, but we don't care.

From rooftops, snowdrops land like dreams,
Carrot noses for lively schemes.
Beneath the surface, a giggle lurks,
In frozen lands where mischief works.

Hot chocolate, slick with twirls and swirls,
Mittens tangled in a dance with whirls.
Each sip's a chuckle, laugh out loud,
In a frosty fun, we all feel proud.

As the sun peeks, and shadows play,
We build our kingdoms, hip hooray!
In the quiet, joy's found anew,
In every flake, a story's due.

Ghosts of Winter's Chill

Bobbing heads of snowmen cheer,
With frosty breath, they draw us near.
The wind whispers jokes in frosty glee,
Not a care for the frigid spree.

Icicles point like ghostly fingers,
Their chilly jokes, each laugh lingers.
Tripping over snowdrifts deep,
In playful spirits, we tumble and leap.

A snowball whizzes, a sudden blitz,
Missed my target, I'm bound to flinch.
Snowflakes giggle, they're light and fleet,
In this brisk chaos we take our seat.

Moonlit beams cast shadows so bright,
While snowmen join in freeze-frame fight.
In winter's chill, laughter's our grace,
Bundle up, it's a merry chase!

Drifting Hues of Winter's Heart

When snowflakes twirl in the air,
They dance like clowns without a care.
Falling fast, they tickle your nose,
Oh, what fun! Now where's my toes?

A snowman wearing my old hat,
Dancing like it's a big old cat.
He's got a smile, but oh dear me,
He looks a bit too much like me!

Snowballs fly like spicy ice cream,
Laughter echoes, what a wild dream.
Warming hearts with frosty delight,
Who knew winter could be so bright?

As we slip and slide, oh what a sight,
Legs flailing round, it's pure delight.
We trip and stumble, yet we still grin,
The joy of snow is where we begin!

Treading Softly on Frozen Dreams

On frosty paths, we skate and slide,
The penguins giggle, we're full of pride.
Each step we take, a playful glide,
With hidden snowballs just to bide.

Our laughter echoes off the trees,
As we dodge snowflakes like busy bees.
Those icy patches claim our shoes,
Let's hope the hot cocoa's worth the blues!

Snow forts built like towering walls,
Hiding from laughter, bouncing balls.
A blizzard rolls in, but we don't fret,
What's winter without a snowy debut? Bet!

With cheeks all rosy and boots so wet,
We dance with frost like a pirouette.
The winter chill can't steal our cheer,
For giggles and snowmen always draw near!

Enshrouded by the Softest Light

A fluff of white on rooftops glows,
As we chase shadows where no one goes.
Our hands all frozen, their tricks unfold,
Making angels – but we can't feel gold!

Sunrise paints the frost like a pro,
As we sip cocoa, all in a row.
The world is a canvas; a snowy delight,
But, oops! I fell! What a silly sight!

Pancake moments with snow for flair,
The dog leaps in, with fur in the air.
Our magical dances in swirling flake,
Oh! Watch out now, give me a break!

But in this wonder, joy's a must,
We'll build a fortress, in snow we trust.
So come join in this frosty spree,
A patchwork quilt of glee for you and me!

A Journey Wrapped in Winter's Veil

A scarf wrapped tight, don't let it slip,
As we sled down hills, oh what a trip!
With every bump, giggles abound,
What makes us laugh? The snow on the ground!

Frosty frolics with friends unite,
Building snowmen, what a sight!
But alas, they topple, oh the dismay,
Who knew a snowball could lead to play?

We've lost our mittens, they took flight,
Floating away like dreams through the night.
With icy fingers, we still rejoice,
For every slip adds to our choice.

So we'll laugh, dance, and share the tales,
Through flurries of fun, where laughter prevails.
Journeying together with spirits high,
Who'd have thought, winter's so spry?

A Tapestry of Soft Chill

Frosty flakes on my nose,
Sneeze, and everyone knows!
Climbing hills that look like cake,
Slip and slide, oh what a mistake!

Snowmen dance with floppy hats,
Cats are plotting their comebacks.
Snowball fights and frozen toes,
Laughing loudly as the cold wind blows.

Echoes Beneath the Snowbound Sky

Wacky scarves like rainbow snakes,
Hot cocoa in my belly wakes;
Sledding down a steepened trail,
Landing in a snowy veil!

Whiskers twitching through the flake,
Chasing bunnies, oh, what a wake!
Giggles echo in the night,
Snowflakes twinkle, what a sight!

Moonlit Dreams on Powdered Streets

Noses cold and cheeks so bright,
Frosty trees in silver light.
Wearing mittens, look so fine,
Fingers warm but style's a crime!

Laughter bounces off the walls,
Tripping over snowball calls.
Under blankets, cozy teams,
Joking wildly 'bout our dreams!

The Calm After the Flurry

Silent town draped white and neat,
Snowflakes seem to dance, oh sweet!
Chilling tales from yesterday,
Laughter lingers as we play.

Whispers float in winter's air,
Stories told in comfy chairs.
With warmth we greet the frosty morn,
Smiles grow wide in hearts reborn!

Echoes of Peace in Frozen Landscapes

The snowflakes dance and twirl so bright,
A penguin slipped, oh what a sight!
Snowballs fly like wishes tossed,
Yet, someone's face was the cost.

Icicles hang like sharp teeth,
As skiers zoom past, beneath their wreath.
Mittens lost, hands turned to frost,
'Twas a fashion choice, or so she boasted.

Snowmen wobbled on not-so-strong legs,
One even hiccupped, what funny gags!
A carrot nose, but what a face,
Did he just sneeze? It's a snowy race!

With laughter ringing through the chill,
Frosty figures dance up the hill.
Though quiet seems the world so wide,
In snowball fights, there's no place to hide.

Painting Solitude in Snowy Hues

A snow-covered bench begs for a seat,
But there's a squirrel nibbling on a treat.
"A nut for my thoughts!" it squeaks with glee,
While snowflakes settle quite peacefully.

A lone boot prints zigzag through the drift,
Where did he run? A gift or a rift?
With each step, a quirky dance unfolds,
Adventures lost, but stories retold.

Snowflakes fall like confetti for fun,
Two snowmen argue about who's got sun.
"Mine's taller!" one claims with a fluffy grin,
"Just wait 'til spring, you'll see who will win!"

Laughter drifts on the whispered air,
As hot cocoa warms up the winter fare.
Hearts are light, as the days grow old,
Who knew winter's grip could be so bold?

Starlit Yetis in the Winter Glow

In moonlit nights, they prance and play,
Yeti fashion contests take the stage today.
With woolly hats and snowball guns,
Who knew they'd also love to run?

"Watch me dance!" one yeti proclaims,
As snow spills out, creating new names.
But clumsy feet can't quite take a stand,
They tumble 'round like a rock band!

Stars above twinkle with delight,
As they challenge each other to a snowball fight.
"Best you bring your warmest gear,
For snowballs will fly, so beware, dear!"

With laughter echoing through the night,
These furry giants find pure delight.
Who'd have thought, snow abounds in cheer,
While myths and truths blend year after year?

Fleeting Time in a Frozen Embrace

Time seems to pause in frosted air,
Where snowmen chase their own despair.
"Why won't it melt?" they sadly plead,
Running from sun like a wild stampede!

A snowflake lands on a frozen nose,
"Am I a decoration?" it slightly doze.
As winter giggles, with mirrored sheen,
They question our sanity if we're keen!

Icicles drip, like time on a spree,
"Oh no, the thaw!" yells a snowman with glee.
Yet amidst the panic, there's laughter bloomed,
In fleeting moments, joy is consumed.

So let us revel in the winters bright,
With chilly hugs and snowball fights.
For every bloom and icy trace,
Comedic bliss we find in this space.

Timeless Moments in a Winter's Night

Chubby snowflakes waltz with glee,
They giggle as they land on me.
A snowman grins with carrot nose,
He's more of a friend than he ever knows.

Children bundled, laughter in air,
They slip and slide without a care.
Hot cocoa spills, a marshmallow fight,
As snowflakes twist in frosty delight.

Sledding down hills like speeds of light,
With every tumble, laughter takes flight.
Frosty whispers, secrets on lips,
As a snowball flies, and friendship dips.

So let us dance in this winter's chill,
With laughter echoing, we won't sit still.
In timeless moments, we find our cheer,
As snowflakes twirl, joy drawing near.

The Stillness of a Softly Falling World

A snowflake whispers, 'Catch me if you can',
But slips through fingers like a tiny fan.
The ground is a canvas, untouched and wide,
Where snowball fights prepare for the ride.

Dogs bound in joy, their tails a blur,
Sliding across drifts with a happy purr.
Every bark erupts into winter's song,
Where even the snow won't last too long.

Hot hands on windows, fogging up dreams,
As snowmen plot all their silly schemes.
With noses so cold and cheeks a bright red,
They laugh at the warmth from snug little beds.

In this world of white, let silliness reign,
With frosted giggles as our only gain.
Each moment becomes a memory bright,
In the stillness where laughter takes flight.

Frostbitten Whispers Beneath the Stars

The stars wink down like playful sprites,
As frosty whispers fill the nights.
Snowmen plotting under candle glow,
Chasing snowflakes in a merry show.

Frolicking rabbits make hurried tracks,
While squirrels chuckle and watch their backs.
Hot cider brews and hiccups of fun,
As snowdrops dance under the oblivious sun.

Snowball muzzles and jokes on lips,
Fluffed up jackets, oh, what silly slips!
Ticklish snow, that tumbles and swirls,
Keeps us all laughing like giddy little girls.

Beneath twinkling stars, we share our dreams,
In this sparkling world, nothing's as it seems.
For every puff of snow, let laughter fill the air,
In frostbitten whispers, we find joy to share.

A Dance with the Snowy Leaves

In a whirl of white, we twirl with grace,
While snowflakes descend like a snowy lace.
We toss and we twirl in a flurry of fun,
As the chilly breeze dances, 'Come join the run!'

The trees wear coats made of sparkling bright,
While we belt out carols all through the night.
Fingers grow numb, but spirits feel high,
As we leap and we spin 'neath the moon in the sky.

A tumble here, and a giggle there,
Snowball fights erupt, but we do not care.
With cheeks all aglow, and noses a suds,
We laugh while attempting to dodge icy buds.

So join this carnival of snowy surprise,
As each flake that lands becomes laughter that flies.
For in this chilly wonderland, pure joy thrives,
As we dance with the leaves and the snow, feeling alive!

Frost Enigma in the Silent Woods

A squirrel dons a tiny hat,
In search of nuts, imagine that!
A snowball fight with birds in flight,
Winter's giggle sparks delight.

The trees wear coats of icy lace,
While rabbits hop with puffed-up grace.
The world looks soft, like whipped-up cream,
What a baffling, frosty dream!

Mice in boots dance on the ground,
Making tracks where none are found.
With each leap and twist they twirl,
Winter's stage, a playful whirl!

In this chill, the laughter rings,
As snowflakes fall like tiny wings.
The frosty air, a giggle spree,
Nature's comedy sets us free!

The Still Call of the Winter Night

A deer in pajamas prances by,
While owls debate the stars in the sky.
Snowflakes twirl in a dizzying dance,
All nature seems to take a chance.

The moon wears a smile, oh so bright,
Illuminating penguins ready for flight.
Their feathered friends take off to roam,
Winter nights feel just like home.

Frosty critters find their tunes,
As choirs sing beneath the moons.
Conductors made of soft, white fluff,
Winter's magic is always enough!

So gather round the fire's glow,
Share stories of each funny show.
With each laugh, the chill disappears,
A warm embrace is what endears.

Serene Moments in a Snowbound Realm

A fox in boots goes on a spree,
Chasing shadows, wild and free.
The snowmen wear a crooked grin,
As kids break out their goofy spins.

Frosty flakes like tiny charms,
Make every bush a thing of arms.
They wave hello, they wish good cheer,
In this snowy wonder sphere.

Hats on bunnies, scarves on bears,
The winter critters start their faires.
Laughter melds with chilly air,
What a crazy world laid bare!

A playful wind carries a song,
As winter frolics all night long.
With every giggle, spirits rise,
In this land of snow, we're wise!

Beneath the Plush White Shroud

A cat in boots sneezes on cue,
While mice sit in a cozy brew.
Hot cocoa spills on winter woes,
As laughter's warmth begins to flow.

Chilly puppies chase their tails,
Through the snow, like furry trails.
They tangle up in snowy fights,
Creating joy in winter nights.

As frost blankets the earth so wide,
Chickadees dress up in style and pride.
Each branch adorned, a festive sight,
Winter's party sparkles bright.

So bundle up and take a peek,
At this wonderland, so unique.
Where every laugh becomes a tune,
In the magic of the winter moon!

Harmony in the Quiet Stillness

A squirrel in a scarf, it struts with flair,
A snowman with a carrot nose, quite rare.
He shimmies and shakes with a goofy grin,
While penguins nearby slip and spin.

The trees wear coats of white so bright,
As children make angels, pure delight.
Mom slips while bringing out hot cocoa cups,
But laughter erupts as she spills on the pups.

The drifts pile high, a perfect fortress,
While foxes play tag; the scene's a burst!
Snowballs fly, giggles fill the air,
A snow-laden fight, not a single care.

So share a chuckle, embrace the cold,
Where frozen adventures are worth more than gold.
In this frosty world, all woes cease,
With joy in the laughter and moments of peace.

Beneath the White Whisper of the Sky

A sneaky snowflake lands on a nose,
While a kitten protests in a coat that's too close.
It pounces on drifts, all fluffy and white,
And catnip dreams dance in the moonlight.

The world slows to whispers wrapped in chill,
Frozen pies stuck atop windowsills.
As icicles hang and the air fills with cheer,
Hot chocolate fights, who built the best sphere?

A rabbit in mittens hops with such glee,
While deer do a jig; oh, what a sight to see!
Snowflakes giggle, and the warmth that we feel,
Is more than just snow; it's the laughter that's real.

So let us rejoice in this frosty sprawl,
Where every frostbite turns giggles into brawl.
In the hush of this wonder, friendships grow,
In the wild dance of winter, we let laughter flow.

Tranquility Wrapped in a Frosty Shroud

A dog wearing boots takes a prance,
While neighbors join in for a snowball dance.
With frosty eyebrows and hats askew,
The joy in each flake is shared by the crew.

In quiet corners, shadows run wild,
Snowmen are tipped, not so well-styled.
The snow plow roars, but giggles arise,
As vehicles skid and humans realize.

The sky glows purple as sunsets ignite,
While laughter erupts amidst the twilight.
A group of penguins, they slide and they slip,
Chasing snowflakes, in a frosty trip.

So cozy we are, wrapped in our gear,
Making memories each wintery year.
In this comic ballet of snowflakes' embrace,
We find warmth in joy and smiles on each face.

Shadows Dancing with the Snowflakes

A raccoon in boots gives the snow a shove,
And spins with delight, what a bouncy love!
Frosty cartoons played on this icy stage,
Where socks on a snowman become quite the rage.

The streetlamps twinkle with snow-covered hats,
While children duel with fluffy snow-splats.
In the backdrop of giggles, the owls hoot clear,
As winter's delight brings us all near.

In this winter's wonder, let silliness flow,
With snowflakes a-dancing, in frosty tableau.
Chasing each other, we laugh and we tease,
A jolly parade wrapped in icy breeze.

So gather your friends for a festive fight,
As shadows and snowflakes twirl through the night.
In this delightful blend of frolic galore,
We celebrate winter, who could ask for more?

Serenity Drifting on Icy Wings

Snowflakes dance, oh what a sight,
Frosty feathers soaring in flight.
Penguins slip, a comical scene,
Ice skating's hard, or so it seems.

Snowmen wobble with carrot noses,
As winter's chill around them dozes.
Hot cocoa spills from frosty mugs,
While kids dive in for snowy hugs.

Boots get stuck, and laughter roars,
A snowball fight erupts outdoors.
Sleds fly high, and so do dreams,
With every tumble, joy redeems.

So raise a glass of warming cheer,
To frosty fun, oh what a year!
For while we giggle through the frost,
We find warm joy in winter's cost.

Muffled Lullabies of the Snowy Night

Whispers of snow in the stillness sing,
As fluffy flakes fall like a soft wing.
Rabbits hop in little jumps,
While snowmen try to stand on lumps.

Snow shovels squeak like rusty doors,
Neighbors chuckle as they explore.
Warm socks peek from bulky boots,
Feet find cozy snowball routes.

Snowflakes tickle noses and cheeks,
Giggles burst in playful peaks.
Winter tales spun by the fire,
With cozy pillows that don't tire.

Around the glow, we share our cheer,
With cups of joy, we hold so dear.
Let laughter melt the icy scene,
As we savor winter's funny sheen.

A World Paused in White Wonder

A blanket of white softens the ground,
Each step yields a silly sound.
Snow drifts bury the neighbor's cat,
While kids imagine ways to chat.

With every fall, a fresh surprise,
As frosty noses meet the skies.
Ducks in snow, oh what a craze,
Quacking tunes in snowy haze.

Hot pies bake, the kitchen's warm,
Snooze alarms like snowflakes swarm.
Outside chaos, but here we stay,
With cocoa dreams to melt away.

As the world slows to a winter glide,
We chuckle at snowmen, filled with pride.
In this pause, we find delight,
Laughing at the wonders of the night.

Dreams Brought by the Falling Snow

Falling flakes sprinkle the ground,
A soft hush, the world unwound.
Through frosted panes, laughter flows,
As winter fun in each heart grows.

Sleds zoom past in wild delight,
Snowball fights turn day to night.
Chirpy birds in winter's chill,
Sing silly songs, we can't sit still.

Snow greet us at every door,
While boots trudge in a snowy chore.
Carrot noses fall askew,
As snowmen grin, feeling brand new.

When morning comes, let's share a laugh,
Building dreams on a snowy path.
With each bite of frosted whim,
Winter's magic lives within.

Silent Drapes of Winter

The flakes fall down like feathers,
As kids run madly, no tether.
Snowmen with noses made from pie,
That melt and drip as time goes by.

A dog prances, tongue out wide,
In pursuit of snowballs, like a slide.
He leaps in joy, then slips and falls,
With snowy face with no recalls.

Cold cheeks and laughter fill the air,
Mittens lost without a care.
Snowflakes dance, but hats fly high,
Good luck, dear hat, on your goodbye!

Yet, snowball fights take playful aim,
Laughter echoes, it's all a game.
But watch your back, or you might find,
A snowball nephew had defined!

Whispers Beneath a Frosty Veil

The world transforms, a clownish sight,
With snowmen wearing underwear tight.
They stand guard with a goofy grin,
'Look at us!' they shout, 'We're made to win!'

A penguin waddle, trip, and crash,
Will he fly? Oh, what a flash!
Slippers on ice, a dance that starts,
To make us giggle with warm hearts.

Sleds zoom down a lumpy hill,
Adults scream loud, it's a thrill;
But if they fall, oh what a scene,
Laughing at each other's green.

And when the day is finally done,
Hot cocoa warms, we're all in fun.
With marshmallows floating snugly near,
"The snow's to blame for all this cheer!"

Dreams Cradled in White

Blankets thick like cakes abound,
Whiskered cats in leaps unbound.
With paws of joy, they bound about,
And faceplant deep in icy pout.

Awkward angels on the ground,
Trying to fly, and yet, they drown.
Their wings of snow all frazzled clumps,
Laughter sparkles, like little lumps.

A snowball toss, a hit in stride,
But then it splats on someone's ride!
With muffled giggles, ducks take flight,
As chaos reigns, it feels just right.

The night winds down, we sip with glee,
Whispers of warmth like family.
In dreams we drift, with cheeks aglow,
'This snow is fun,' we softly show.

When the World Wears a Blanket

The sky is gray, a lazy sheet,
Little toes in fuzzy heat.
Hot chocolate swirls, the marshmallows swim,
As toes start tapping to winter whim.

With every flake, a giggle grows,
The world outside is a comedy show.
Carrots for noses are oh-so silly,
While penguins slide in a playful frilly.

Kids tumble down hills with squeaky shrieks,
While snowmen plead, 'Give us some tweaks!'
As squirrels wear scarves and play around,
A topsy-turvy winter playground!

So let us laugh 'neath this fluffy quilt,
Where joy multiplies, and worries wilt.
Crafts of snow, with each chuckle spun,
In this frosty world, we have such fun!

The Lullaby of Falling White

Flakes fall down, soft as a cat,
Whispering secrets, where's my hat?
Snowmen grinning, looking so fine,
Lost in giggles, sipping on brine.

Sleds are whizzing, parents all scream,
Riders fly off, oh, what a dream!
Frosty friends with carrot noses,
Tickle your ribs, then strike poses.

Hot cocoa waiting, marshmallows dance,
Snowball fights break out by chance.
Slip on the sidewalk, down you go,
Covered in laughter, we steal the show.

Blankets of white, silly and grand,
Making us giggle, hand in hand.
Under the skies, full of delight,
The lullaby whispers all through the night.

Ghostly Steps on Whispering Snow

Footprints shuffle, oh what a sight,
Ghosts in the night, chasing the light.
But it's just kids, all bundled tight,
Slipping and sliding with no sense of fright.

Whispers of snow, secrets unfold,
Chasing their shadows, oh so bold.
Snowflakes are laughing, giggling so clear,
Calling us all, come have no fear.

Chill in the morning, warm hearts ignite,
Falling down softly, in pure delight.
Imaginary friends wave us on,
While we blissfully play until dawn.

What tales will the frost share tonight?
With icy giggles, soft as moonlight.
Through all the chase, laughter will flow,
In a cold world, we glow and we grow.

A Crypt of Secrets in Icy Gleams

A sparkly world, under a glaze,
Mice take a stroll in their tiny haze.
Snowflakes whisper and giggle aloud,
As snowmen party, jolly and proud.

With every flake that tickles our nose,
Comes the laughter, and in comes the prose.
Sleds down the hills, gravity's tease,
While hot chocolate waits, bringing us ease.

Shadows of snow, we run and we play,
Creation's delight, melting away.
What crispy concoction does winter bestow?
A crypt of laughter, wrapped in the glow.

So here we are, let's dance and skate,
With friends by our side, let's celebrate.
Chilled as we are, our giggles ignite,
In a world of white, everything feels right.

Veiled Journeys on a Frosty Path

Shimmering trails, soft whispers of ice,
A leap, a tumble, oh, isn't that nice?
Frosty old trees, with secrets so deep,
Hide giggling elves who can't even sleep.

Chasing their tails, or maybe a hat,
Snowball shenanigans, where's my spat?
Through twinkling nights, we make our mark,
Creating mischief, igniting a spark.

Each corner turned, brings laughter anew,
Ice skating trips, with friends, just a few.
Snowmen in hats looking quite dapper,
While we all giggle, and giggle, and caper.

Veiled journeys call to the wild and the bold,
With every soft flake, a story unfolds.
Snowflakes can't help, but twirl and sway,
As we dance through the night, in winter's ballet.

Reflections Beneath the Winter's Warmth

A snowman wearing a top hat,
With a carrot nose that's gone flat.
His smile is big, but wait, oh dear!
Is that a squirrel stealing his ear?

Children slide with giggles so bright,
On a hill that's just sheer delight.
While parents sip cocoa, hands in mitts,
Worrying about those infamous splits.

The dog jumps high, he thinks he's a star,
Chasing his tail like a fuzzy bazaar.
In every snowball, laughter ignites,
Winter's a stage with silly delights.

As snowflakes dance from the sky's loop,
We'll all gather 'round for a warm soup.
So here's a cheer to the frosty plot,
With snowmen, chuckles, and a hot cocoa pot!

Glimmers of Peace in Frozen Fields

Pigeons wobble on icy grey,
Look at them dance, they're on display!
A fluff ball cat, with a pounce so spry,
Mistakes the snow for a fluffy pie.

A rogue snowflake lands on my nose,
Tickles and giggles, where laughter flows.
With every slip and every glide,
We're wondering who will fall, not slide.

The sleds go zoom with a jolly cheer,
While hot chocolate waits, ever near.
With whipped cream mountains taking the stage,
We all gather 'round, to laugh and engage.

So let the winter's humor unfold,
In fields so white, where fun is bold.
We'll share in the joy of life's little quirks,
And laugh at the snow's whimsical smirks!

Tranquil Footprints in a Cottoned Twilight

Footprints lead through glittering white,
Where squirrels plot mischief in the night.
A duck in a scarf goes waddling past,
Wondering if a snowball might last.

Snowflakes twirl in a comical ballet,
As kids find ways to tumble and sway.
With a winter coat that's two sizes too big,
One child ninja-rolls past a snow pig.

A snowball fight breaks out with a cheer,
Faces turn red, but laughter is near.
Beware of the snowmen, they throw ice too!
Their carrot noses are armed and ready to skew.

In the twilight glow, a snow angel lies,
With wings spread wide, under starry skies.
We'll laugh and play till the day is done,
In this sparkly world, we're all bound to have fun!

The Hidden Life Beneath the Chill

In shadows, rabbits plot their great schemes,
While icicles glimmer with frosty beams.
Nests in the eaves, all cozy and snug,
Winter's embrace like a great, warm hug.

A walrus in skates falls flat on his face,
As we're all doubled over, a hilarious case.
Snowflakes giggle as they fall to the ground,
Whispering secrets in a hush all around.

The wind plays tricks, a jolly old ghost,
Whistling through trees, it seems to boast.
Every snow-covered branch, a soft laugh,
Nature's humor, what a delightful gaffe!

So here's to the frosty, the icy delight,
Where laughter and warmth weave in every night.
Embrace the chill, let the fun times roll,
In this winter tale, let's all warm our soul!

Chilling Dreams on a Moonlit Night

A snowman told a joke, quite bold,
His carrots danced, tales of ice were told.
Yet, he slipped on his own frosty feet,
Laughter echoed, no one faced defeat.

Snowflakes twirled, a waltz on cue,
A cat launched a snowball—who knew?
The dogs caught it, making a mess,
Chasing tails in the winter's dress.

Are those rabbits wearing hats, I swear?
They sip hot cocoa, quite the pair!
Laughter in the chilly air,
As snowflakes twinkle without a care.

The moon chuckled, a shining grin,
Gossiping with shadows, their nightly spin.
In the frost-kissed night, joy takes flight,
Chilling dreams burst in playful delight.

Silence Cloaked in Crystal Blankets

Snow drifts whisper, secrets so bright,
Squirrels in pajamas, oh what a sight!
A bunny hops, wearing boots too large,
Spring seems far, but winter's in charge.

Icicles hang like crystals in a row,
While penguins slide—oh, the show!
With a fluffle and a flutter, they make a scene,
Adventurers bold, in a landscape pristine.

Frosty friends in a dance divine,
They twirl and glide on a frosted line.
With each slip and slide, a giggle escapes,
Snowmen planning winter capes!

Laughter rings out from the snowy glade,
As chili-eating penguins parade!
In this frozen realm, joy ignites,
Silence teem with snowy delights.

Frozen Petals in a Shimmering World

The roses wrapped in winter's lace,
Giggle softly, in this white embrace.
With heav'nly scents, they dance in place,
While snowflakes pirouette in a wild race.

Tulip hats and daisy gloves,
Garden sprites made of icy loves.
They sip their tea from a frozen cup,
A toast to winter, let's live it up!

Snow's a canvas for tricks and pranks,
Slipping gnomes in chilly ranks.
The squirrels with acorns, a part-time show,
As winter winds whisper, "Ho, ho, ho!"

Yet, beneath this blanket, a soft laugh lies,
As winter dances beneath ink-black skies.
Frozen petals, so bright and bold,
In this glittering world, warmth unfolds.

The Soft Caress of Winter's Breath

Frosty kisses ride on the wind,
While polar bears break into a spin.
Sliding in socks, oh what a sight,
Each tumble a tumble, each fall a delight!

The trees are tickled, their branches sway,
Jokes bouncing like balls in a merry play.
An owl snores loudly, what a trip,
Winter's lullabies rock him to sleep!

Flakes flutter down like confetti bright,
As snowmen giggle in pure delight.
They play hide and seek, oh what a spree,
In a world where fun sets every heart free!

Laughter veils the frosty air,
Winter's breath plays without a care.
In this chilly haven, joy finds a way,
As soft lights dance on a snowy play.

Echoes of the Snowbound Heart

A snowman grins with a carrot nose,
His buttons droop, and everyone knows.
He tells bad jokes, but we can't complain,
Laughter erupts like sunshine in rain.

The dog takes a leap, but he miscalculates,
He jumps for a snowball, oh, the fates!
He lands in a mound, it's a sight to see,
Covered in snow, he looks quite happy!

Kids throw snowflakes like they're confetti,
But their aim is off, oh, they're not ready.
One hits the dad, who just can't take it,
He slips on the ice—he can't quite shake it!

As we laugh and play, the warm cocoa calls,
A fort of snowballs, let's see who falls!
The world is a blanket, cozy and bright,
In this winter wonder, we find pure delight.

Illuminated by the Frosty Moon

The moon hangs low, a cheeky bright light,
It nudges the stars with giggles at night.
Frosty whispers create a soft sound,
As snowflakes tango, all twirling around.

A squirrel in boots skitters with flair,
Executing flips, with nary a care.
He snatches a nut, then suddenly slips,
Down the tree trunk, he cartwheels and flips!

We build a chalet, with pillows and sheets,
Impromptu camping, quite a silly feat.
As we toast marshmallows, laughter ignites,
The fire crackles with fun, joyful nights.

In this snowy world, let whimsy take hold,
With cocoa mustaches and hearts made of gold.
Each star is a wink, each flake a delight,
Under the moonlight, we embrace the night.

Blossoms of Hushed Winter's Breath

The frost on the branches creates a scene,
Like glittery flowers, all sparkly and green.
A bear in a sweater strolls down the lane,
Plotting a snowball fight, oh, what a game!

The penguins parade, all waddling small,
In their little tuxedos, they stand up tall.
They're planning a dance, but how can they strut?
With one little slip, they've all gone kaput!

A raccoon in mittens finds cookies galore,
He munches and crunches, then looks for more.
His eyes dance with glee, oh what a sight,
As he takes his haul, sneaky in the night.

With laughter that rings through the chilly air,
Where everything's coated, and joy is laid bare.
In the hush of the season, let fun take the lead,
For these blossoms of humor are all that we need.

Reflections in a Blanket of Snow

Reflections emerge, in this frosty retreat,
A kid on a sled, oh, feeling the heat!
He zooms down the hill, a blur in the white,
But stops dead in tracks at a snowball fight!

A family of ducks waddle, quack, and slip,
On ice-coated ponds, oh, what would they trip?
One takes a tumble and plops with a splash,
Now everyone's laughing; oh, what a crash!

As snowflakes flutter like popcorn in air,
A snow angel flops, with the grace of a bear.
With arms flailing wildly in topsy-turvy style,
She's crowned as the queen, with a snow-covered smile.

So gather your friends, let the giggles unfold,
In this winter wonder, the stories retold.
Each flake is a memory, each laugh brings us cheer,
As we bask in the joy that this season holds dear.

Wrapped in a Gentle Chill

Flakes descend like cotton candy,
Covering all in a fluffy coat.
Sleds zoom past in a merry race,
While snowmen dance in their frosty lace.

Birds in hats, oh what a sight!
They chirp and chirp, giving quite a fright.
Hot cocoa spills from smiles so wide,
As we slip and slide, what a goofy ride!

Children giggle, doggies prance,
In a winter wonderland of pure chance.
Laughter echoes through the trees,
With snowflakes tickling like nippy breeze.

So let the cold wrap 'round us tight,
With giggles echoing all through the night.
For in this chill that seems so stark,
We find our joy, like a bright, warm spark.

Heartbeats in the Frozen Landscape

Puffy jackets bobbing up and down,
As snowballs fly all over town.
With pink noses and cheeks aglow,
We stumble about, just look at us go!

Frosty breath mingling with the air,
Our laughter floats, free as a spare.
Penguin waddles, oh what a sight,
As we trip and fall with all our might!

Snowflakes catching on our tongues,
We sing loud songs that must be sung.
An army of snowmen standing tall,
With snowballs ready, we'll have a ball!

So let's embrace this frosty spree,
With every giggle, just you and me.
In this wintry mischief, pure delight,
We keep our heartbeats warm and bright.

The Stillness That Follows

Shhh, listen closely, can you hear?
The whisper of snowflakes falling near.
In the quiet, a snowflake sneezed,
With a gentle giggle, winter's pleased!

Squirrels hide nuts for the icy days,
While snowmen plot their tricky ways.
"Catch me if you can!" they seem to say,
As we slip and slide, all in play.

The air is crisp, the world aglow,
Footprints lead where no one can go.
And with a push, a snowball flies,
A surprise attack, the kids all rise!

Inside, we sip a steamy drink,
While outside blizzards make us think.
Of warmth to come when fun's all done,
In the stillness, we've just begun.

Solitude Adorned in White

Cocooned in layers, feeling so bold,
With snow-pants on, a sight to behold.
Wandering solo, but never alone,
With giggles echoing, a joyful tone.

Icicles hang, like teacher's rulers,
While I dodge the puddles, like silly fools.
A snow-flap here and a frosty paw,
Nature watching with one big "Ha-ha!"

Cardigan wearing, mittens so nice,
Every snowflake, a discreet slice.
In solitude, I find my cheer,
As laughter floats from far and near.

With twirls and leaps, I join the dance,
In a frozen world, we take our chance.
For every drift and pile of snow,
Brings joy and laughter, let it flow!

A Symphony in Frost and Stillness

In fluffy coats we waddle, oh so round,
With icy noses bumping on the ground.
The snowflakes dance, a whimsical parade,
While penguins slip, our laughter serenade.

Sleds fly by, with giggles in the air,
We tumble down, without a single care.
Hot cocoa waits, with marshmallows afloat,
But first another snowball must be shot!

Snowmen sporting hats a size too big,
Mufflers wrapped, they strut a frozen jig.
The frost is fierce, yet spirits lift on high,
As snowflakes fall, we reach for the sky.

The winter tunes, they hum a merry tune,
As toes go numb beneath the bright, full moon.
In this frosty realm, joy's never shy,
With every flake, our worries slip on by.

Moments Suspended in the Snowfall

Snowballs fly, a flurry of delight,
We make a mess, but nothing's quite so bright.
A snowman stands, arms raised in pure glee,
While squirrels sneak snacks; oh, what a spree!

Our laughter echoes, a chorus so sweet,
As mittens clash in a giant snowball feat.
Gloves now soaked, a fashion statement bold,
But warmth will come, or so I've been told.

Snowflakes tickle noses, a playful tease,
Each one's unique, like family with ease.
We whirl and twirl in this frosty domain,
Wishing forever this fun won't wane.

As icicles dangle, a crystal display,
We race and tumble, come what may.
Winter whispers, but all we can hear,
Is laughter and joy, our hearts sincere.

Whispers Beneath the Frosted Veil

Beneath all the white, mischief does dwell,
As secret snowballs prepare quite a spell.
A rumble of giggles runs soft in the night,
While parents insist it's a peaceful sight.

In winter's embrace, we sneak to and fro,
Pancakes for breakfast, topped high with snow.
A snowman's hat made from a big ol' pot,
Can't tell if he's cool, or just forgot!

The frost pulls at cheeks, a chilly embrace,
While the dog joins in, ready to chase.
He leaps and he bounds, all furry and fast,
Snowflakes a flurry, a wintery blast!

Together we build, a fortress of fun,
With battles of snow, till the day is done.
Under the glow, as the stars start to peep,
We giggle and tumble, then drift off to sleep.

Secrets Wrapped in Winter's Embrace

In piles of white, we find our joy expressed,
Chasing our shadows, each other, we jest.
Snowflakes catchers with sticks in our hands,
Exchanging whispers in this snowy land.

A snow angel here, a flop there, we laugh,
Creating memories on this chilly path.
The world turns soft, like a blanket of cream,
We skip and we twirl, lost in a dream.

Earmuffs oversized, we don't really care,
As our cheeks turn pink, with frost in the air.
The dog pulls a sled, slipping on ice,
With every wild turn, our hearts feel so nice.

With hot drinks waiting, our spirits will lift,
A world full of wonders, all wrapped up in drift.
In snowball fights, we lose track of the hour,
In winter's giggles, we find all our power.

Milton Keynes UK
Ingram Content Group UK Ltd.
UKHW022007131124
451149UK00013B/1056